SPOOKY OOKY

AND THE DISAPEARING COOKIES

SIONNA SILVER

THANK YOU FOR
READING!

SPOOKY OOKY AND THE MYSTERIOUS MISSING COOKIES

On Halloween night when
the moon is in the sky,
Spooky Ooky and
his daddy float on by.

They lived in a house that
would send shivers up
your spine.

His little brown dog
followed them
everywhere. He had the
spookiest
"A-WOOOOOOO".

The ghosts of
the town flew
through the sky
as little
"boooo's" trailed
behind.

Spooky Ooky was excited to
get home. His mommy had
made spooky cookies special
for him.
Skeletons, aliens, and even
kittens too!

He rushed home and
flew as fast as he
could, hovering over
the land below.

As he got close to the
house he could smell the
cookies fresh out of the
oven.

But...

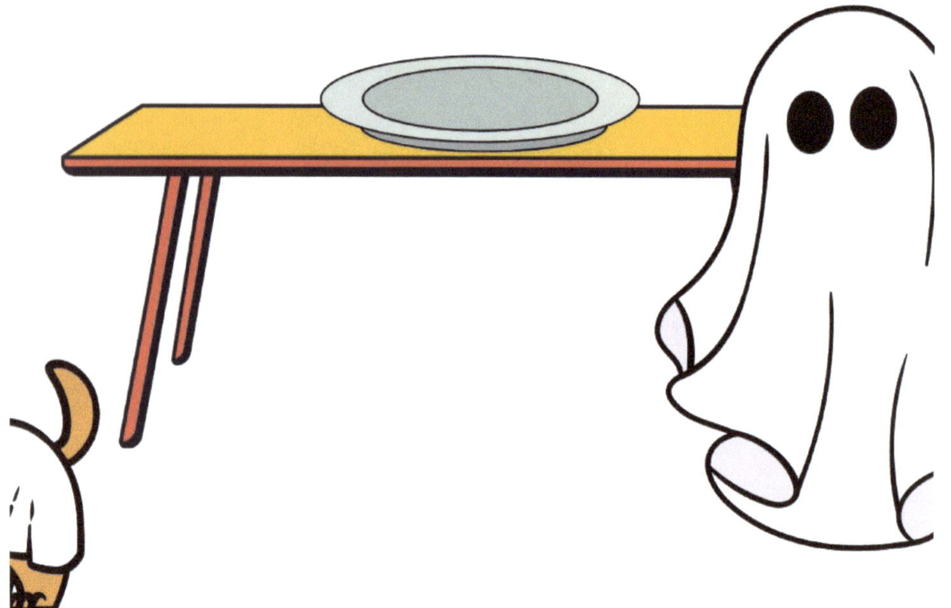

when he got to the kitchen
all of the cookies were gone!
There were no skeletons,
aliens or kittens left.

The little ghost bursted into tears!

Where had they gone?
Who could've taken
them all?

Spooky Ooky put on his detective outfit and determined it was time to solve the mystery.

But how?! Who else could have possibly been in the kitchen?

He quickly looked
around the house
to see if the cookie
theif was still
around.

There was no one in the living
room, not even a crumb. The
little ghost continued on.

He ran into his mommy
down the hall.
"Mommy ghost did you
eat all the cookies?"
Spooky Ooky asked.

"No, not I." mommy ghost
replied. He began to worry
but there was still hope.

Spooky Ooky
ventured outside.
He asked the wise
old owl, "Have you
seen my cookies?"

"Hoo-hoo! Not I."
They replied.

He stumbled a
crossed a little
black cat in a
witches hat.

"Have you seen
my cookies?"
The little ghost
asked.

"Not I." said the
black cat.

He ran into the little witch
who lived down the street.
"Excuse me,
have you seen my cookies?"

"No, not I." said the little
witch. "But i sense they are
very close by."

The little ghost
looked
everywhere
under the
moon. He knew
it was bed time
soon.

He went back to the house
and sat for a minute. He
could still smell the
cookies in the air.

The little ghost was
so sad. He's always
had them on
Halloween night!

It wasn't Mommy
ghost, or the owl.
Not the cat or the
witch.

Just then he
heard it.

The spookiest
little...

"AWOOOOOOOOO!"

The spooky
little dog had a
bucket of
goodies!

But what was
inside?

The little ghost could not believe his eyes! The spooky cookies were in the bucket, gently placed side by side.

Spooky Ooky began to cry again, but this time for joy. His best friend had been carrying the cookies the whole time.

He ate his cookies, and
gave his little dog a
bone.

What an adventure he had!
He was sad it had to end.
The little ghost headed
home...

With his belly full of cookies, and with his very best friend.

Thanks for reading.

Watch for the next boo-k!